FIVE
5
FINGER
IANO

FIRST POP SONGS

ISBN 978-1-4803-6188-1

HAL•LEONARD®
CORPORATION

7777 W. BLUEMOUND RD. P.O. BOX 13819 MILWAUKEE, WI 53213

Visit Hal Leonard Online at
www.halleonard.com

CONTENTS

Tears in Heaven

Words and Music by Eric Clapton
and Will Jennings

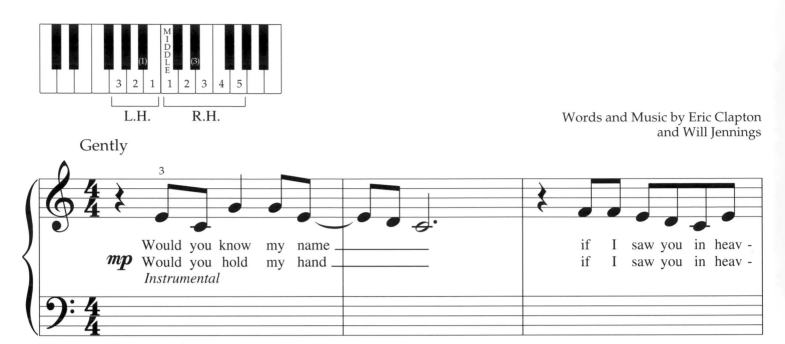

Gently

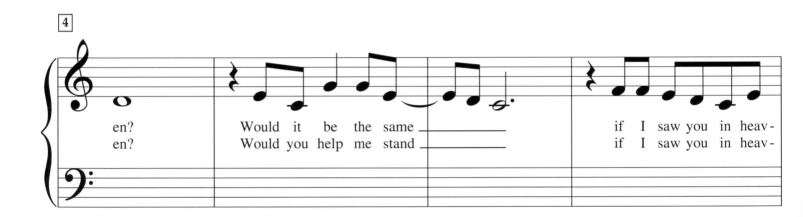

Duet Part (Student plays one octave higher than written.)

Gently

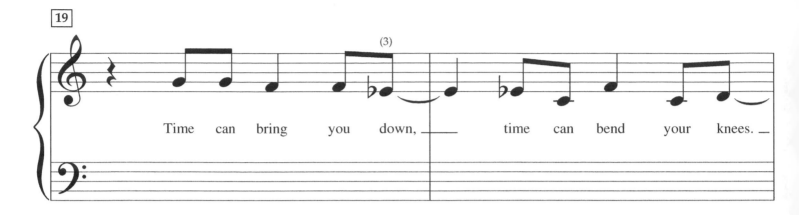

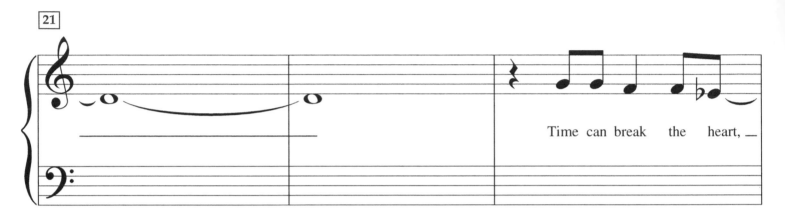

Candle in the Wind

Words and Music by Elton John
and Bernie Taupin

Duet Part (Student plays one octave higher than written.)

Lean on Me

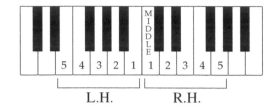

Words and Music by
Bill Withers

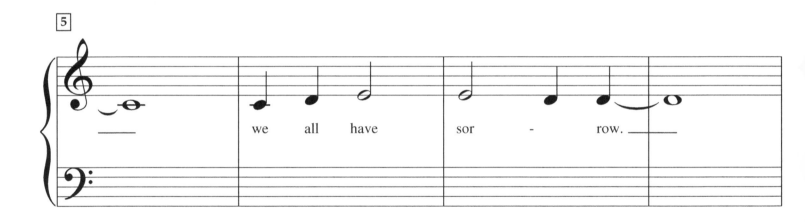

Duet Part (Student plays one octave higher than written.)

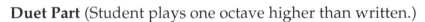

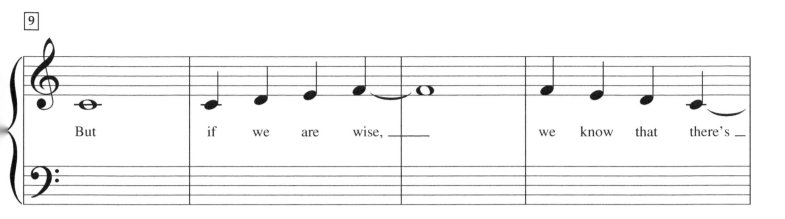

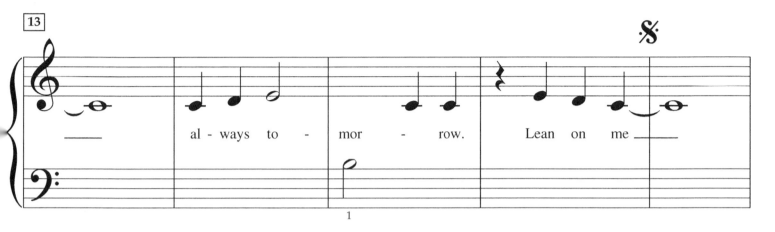

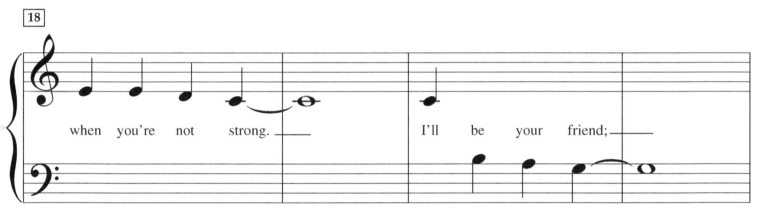

11

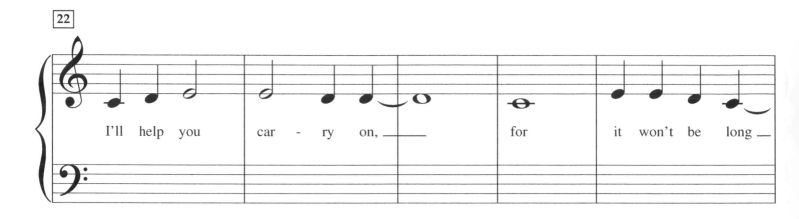

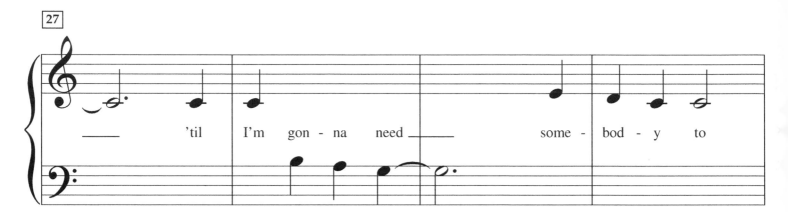

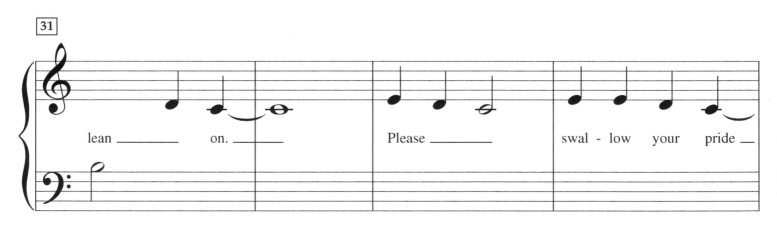

12

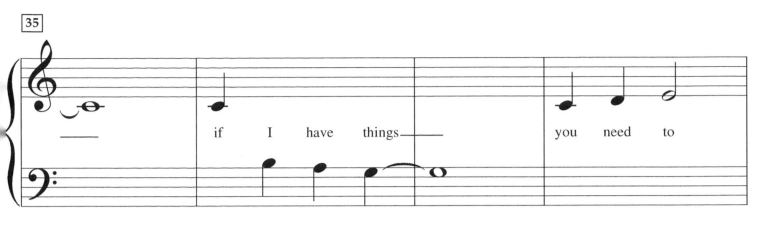

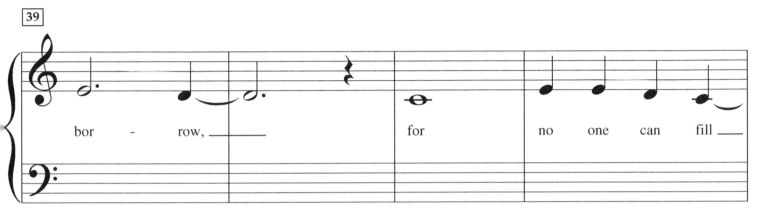

let _____ show. ___ You just call on me, broth - er, when

you need a hand. ___ We all ___ need some-bod - y to lean _

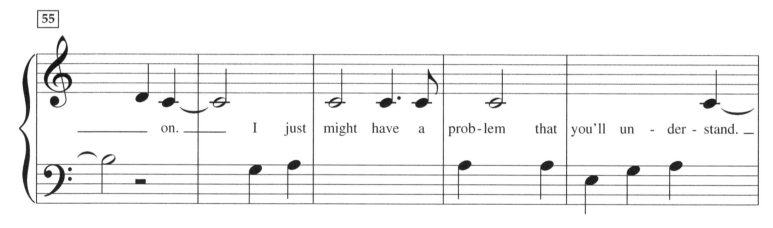

_____ on. ___ I just might have a prob-lem that you'll un - der-stand. _

14

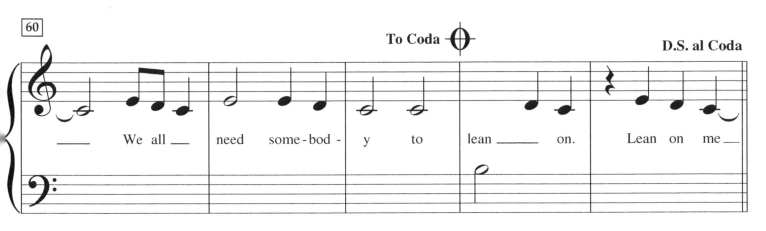

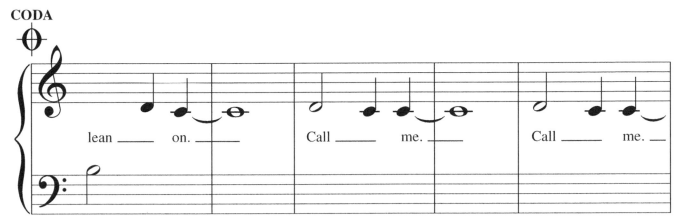

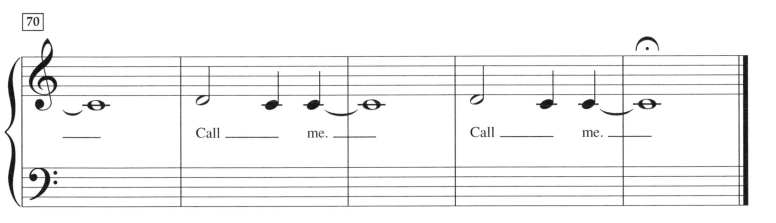

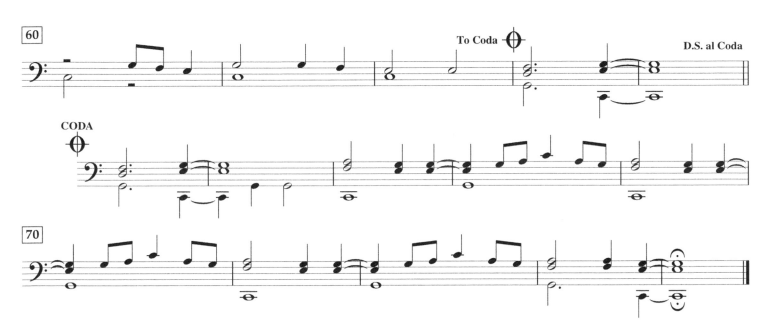

Moon River
from the Paramount Picture BREAKFAST AT TIFFANY'S

Words by Johnny Mercer
Music by Henry Mancini

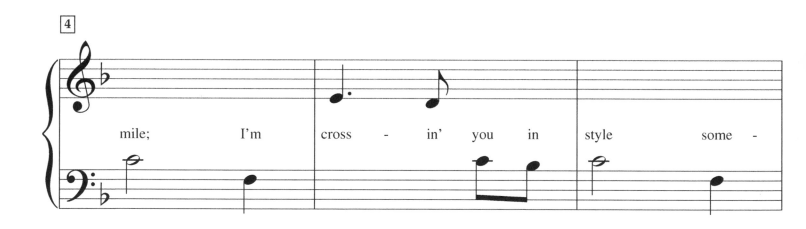

Duet Part (Student plays one octave higher than written.)

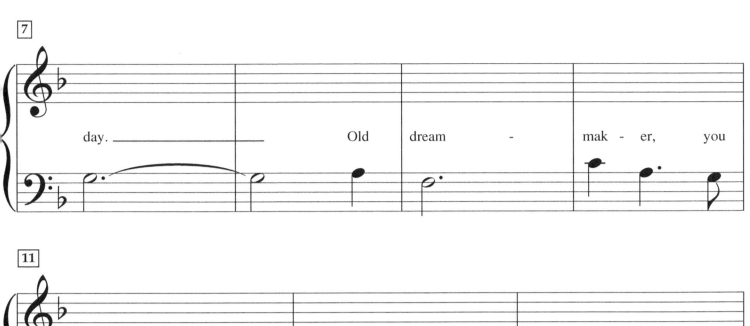

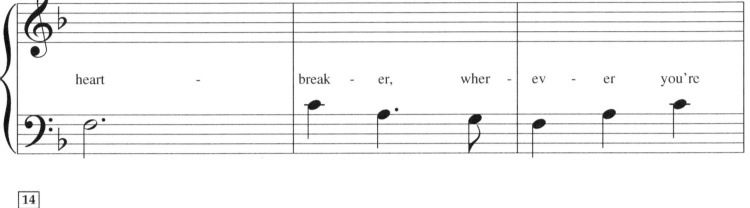

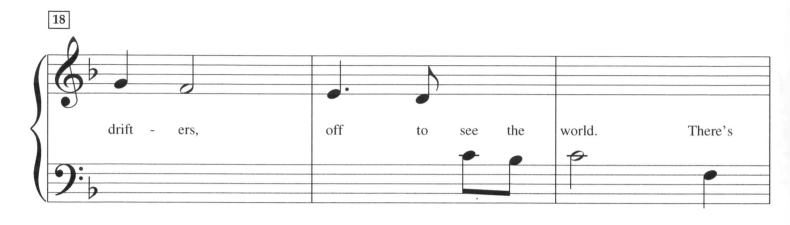

drift - ers,   off   to   see   the   world.   There's

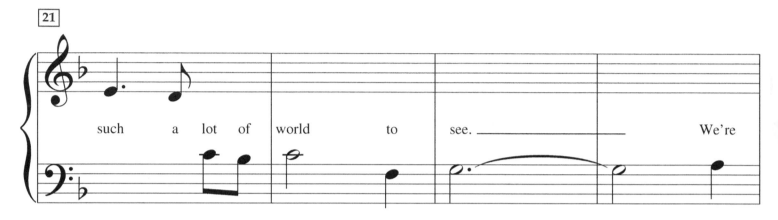

such   a   lot of   world   to   see. _____   We're

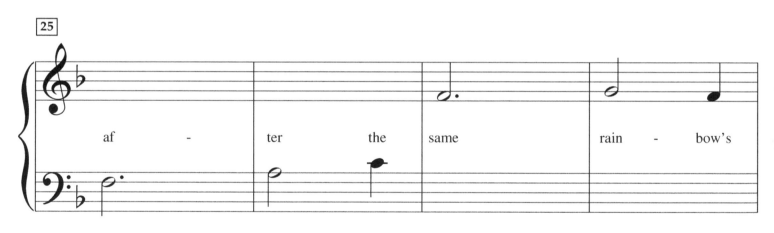

af -   ter   the   same   rain -   bow's

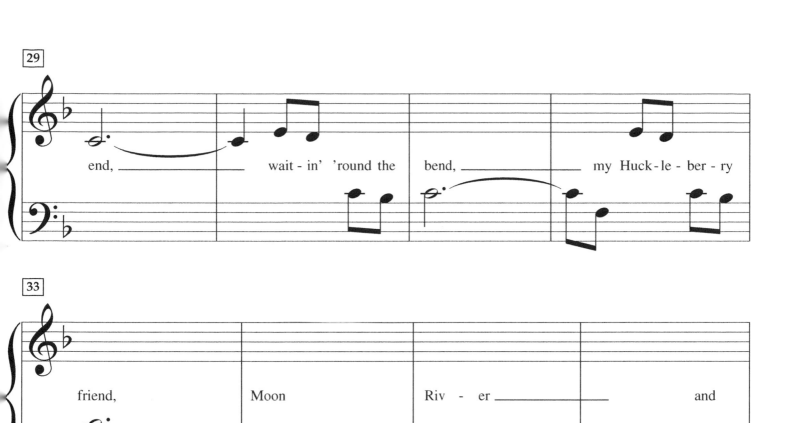

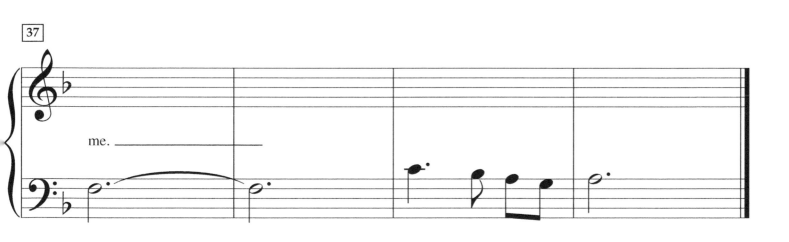

19

Piano Man

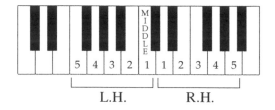

Words and Music by
Billy Joel

Moderately fast

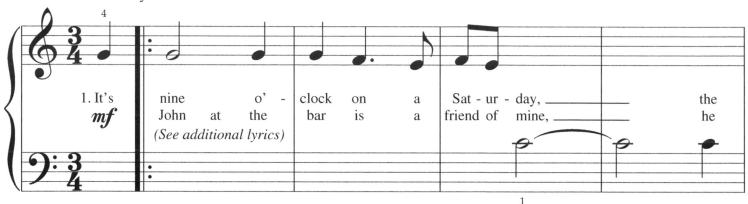

1. It's nine o' - clock on a Sat - ur - day, _____ the
John at the bar is a friend of mine, _____ he

mf

(See additional lyrics)

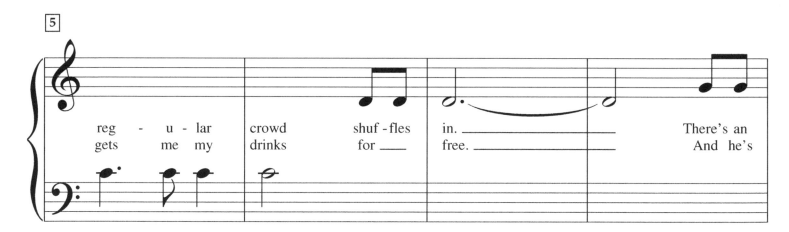

reg - u - lar crowd shuf -fles in. _____ There's an
gets me my drinks for ___ free. _____ And he's

Duet Part (Student plays one octave higher than written.)

Moderately fast

mp

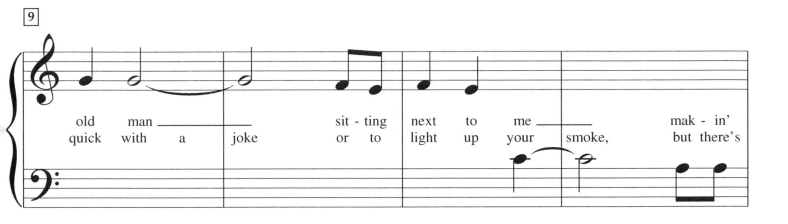

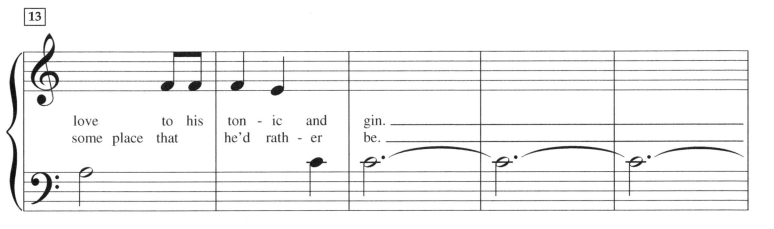

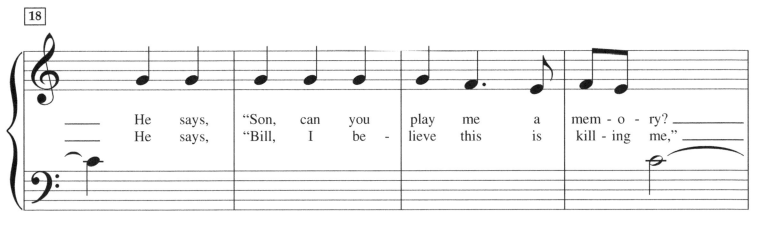

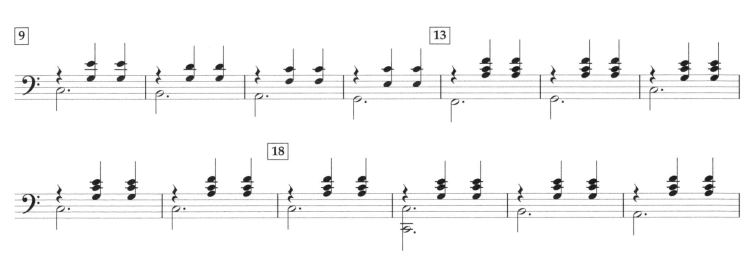

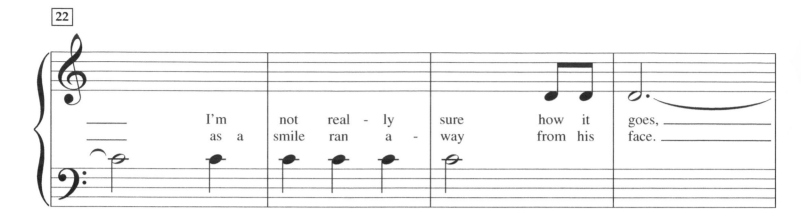

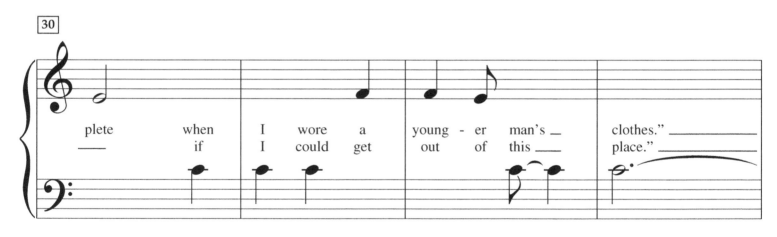

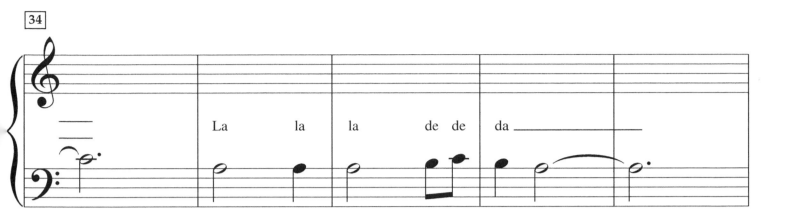

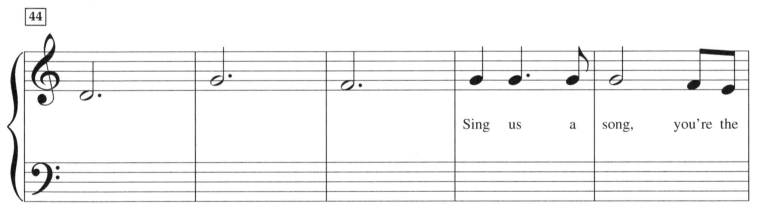

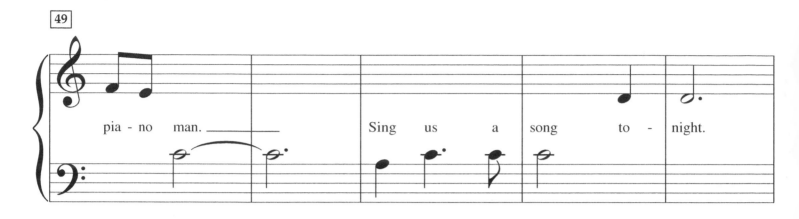

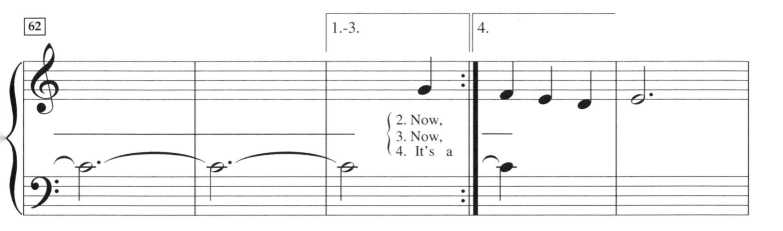

Additional Lyrics

3. Now, Paul is a real estate novelist, who never had time for a wife
   And he's talkin' with Davy, who's still in the Navy, and probably will be for life.
   And the waitress is practicing politics as the businessmen slowly get stoned.
   Yes, they're sharing a drink they call loneliness but it's better than drinkin' alone.

4. It's a pretty good crowd for a Saturday, and the manager gives me a smile
   'Cause he knows that it's me they've been comin' to see to forget about life for a while.
   And the piano, it sounds like a carnival, and the microphone smells like a beer,
   And they sit at the bar and put bread in my jar and say, "Man, what are you doin' here?"

Unchained Melody

from the Motion Picture UNCHAINED

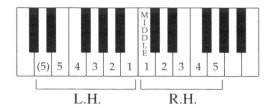

Lyric by Hy Zaret
Music by Alex North

Tenderly

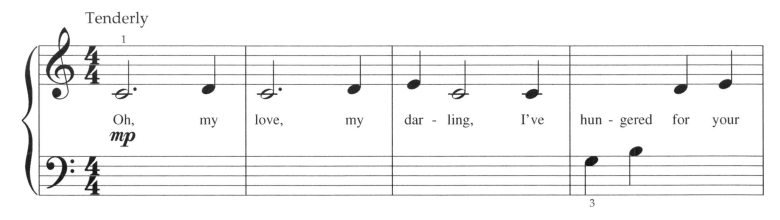

Oh, my love, my dar - ling, I've hun - gered for your

touch a long, lone - ly time. _____

Duet Part (Student plays one octave higher than written.)

Tenderly

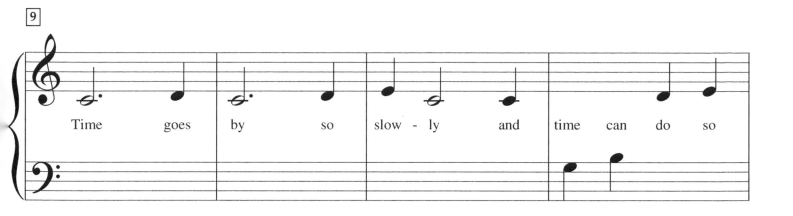

Time goes by so slow - ly and time can do so

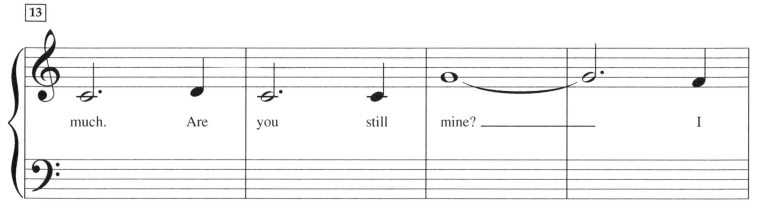

much. Are you still mine? _____ I

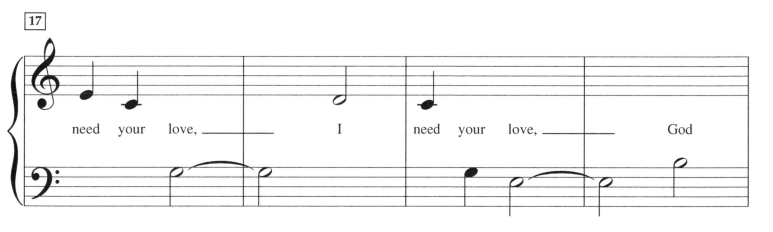

need your love, _____ I need your love, _____ God

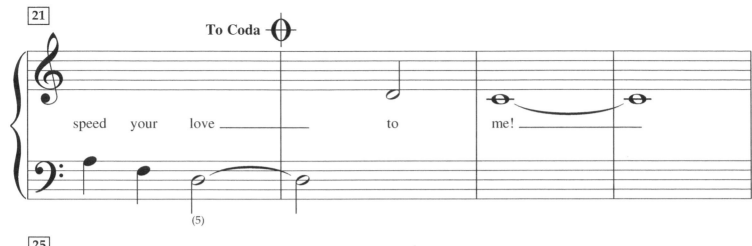

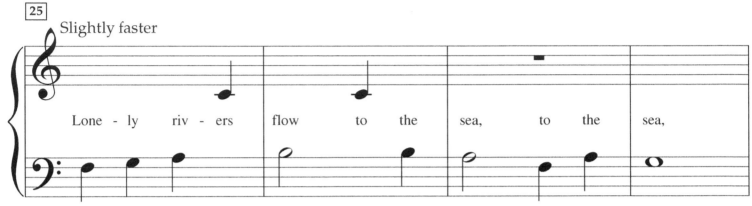

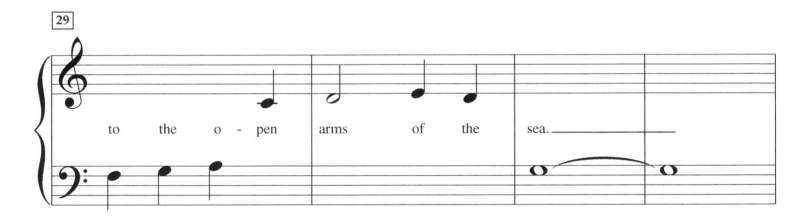

Lone - ly riv - ers sigh, "Wait for me, wait for me!"

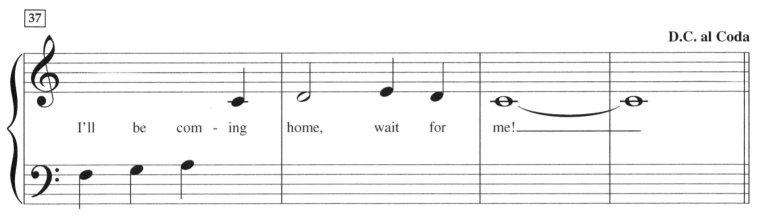

D.C. al Coda

I'll be com - ing home, wait for me!_____

CODA

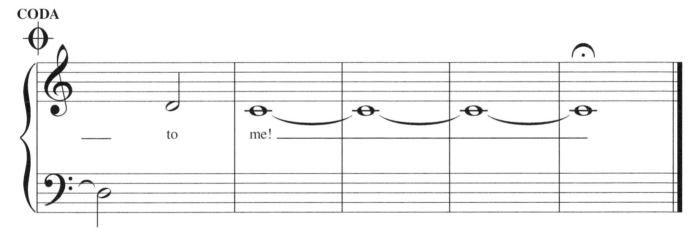

___ to me!_____

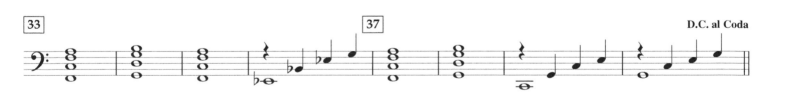

D.C. al Coda

CODA

8vb

Yellow Submarine

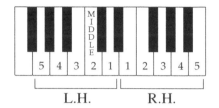

Words and Music by John Lennon
and Paul McCartney

March

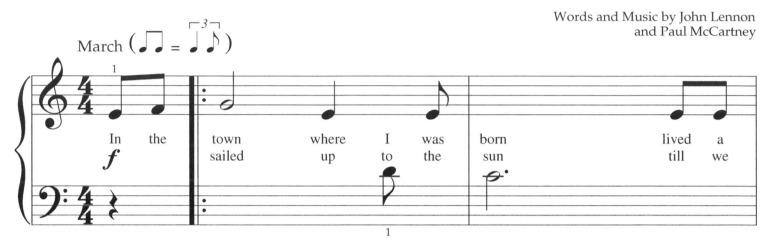

In the town where I was born lived a
sailed up to the sun till we

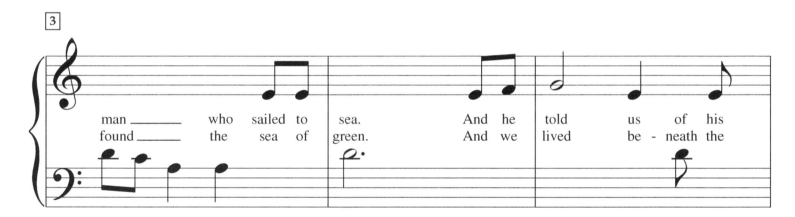

man _____ who sailed to sea. And he told us of his
found _____ the sea of green. And we lived be - neath the

Duet Part (Student plays one octave higher than written.)

March

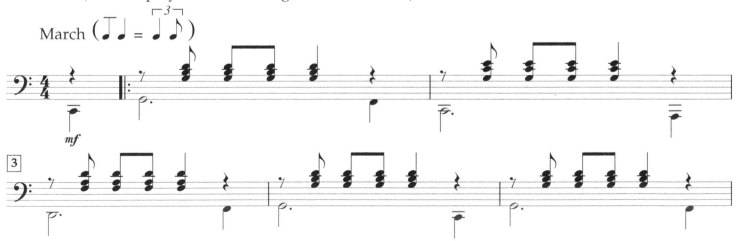

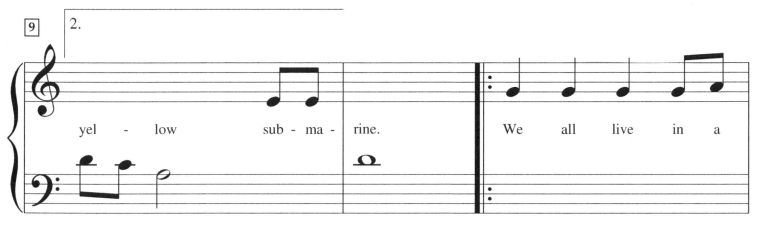

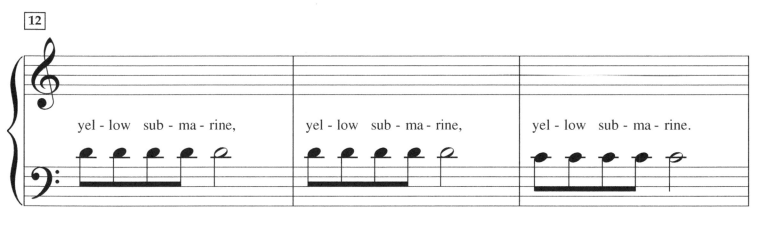

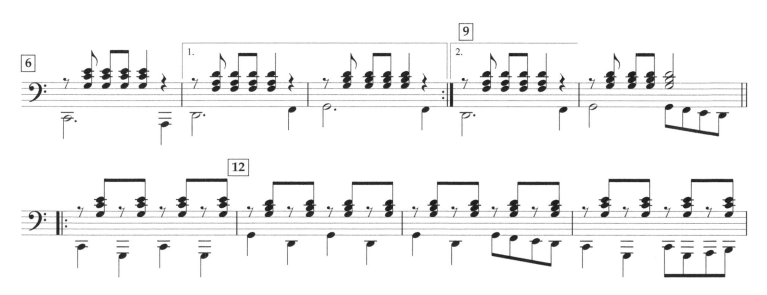

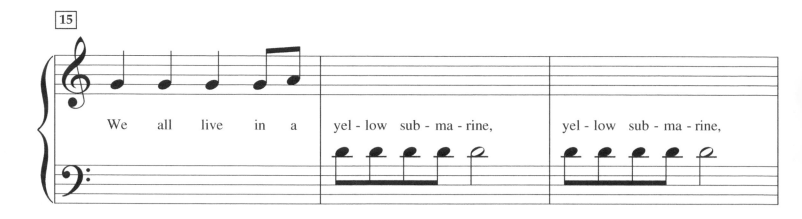

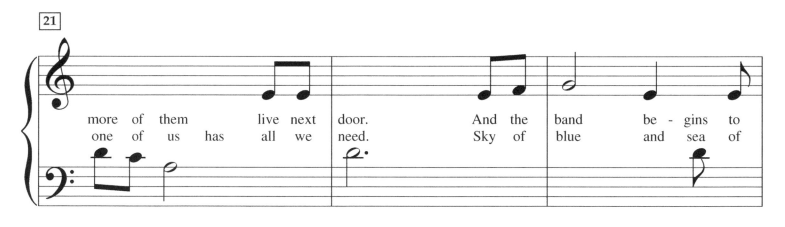

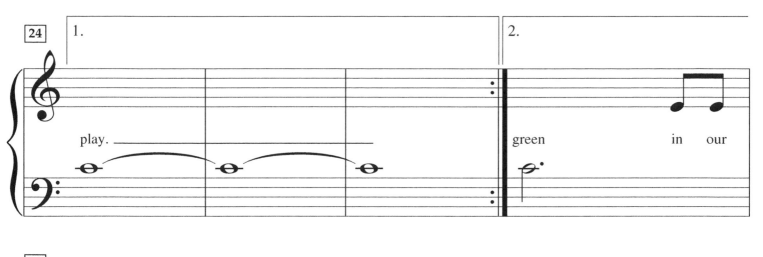

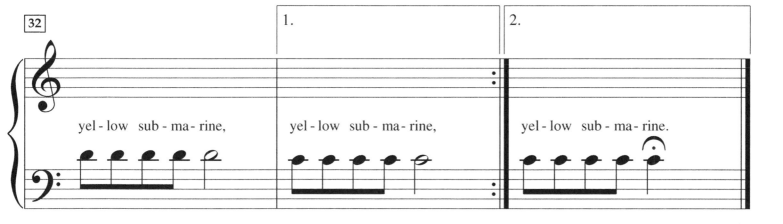

What a Wonderful World

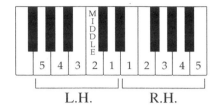

Words and Music by George David Weiss
and Bob Thiele

Moderately, with expression

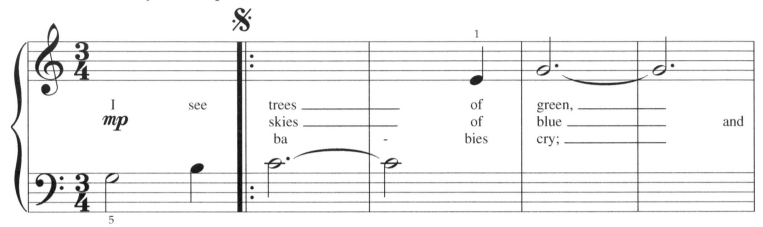

Duet Part (Student plays one octave higher than written.)

Moderately, with expression

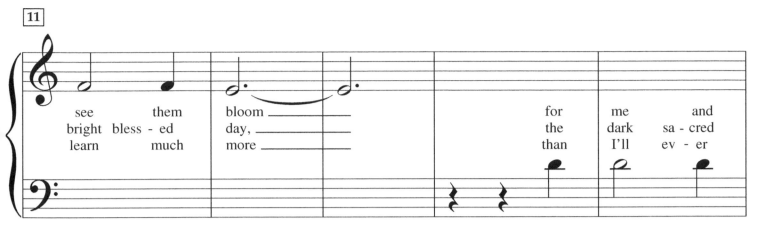

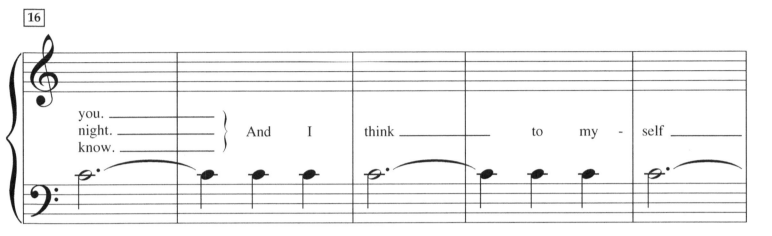

To Coda ⊕

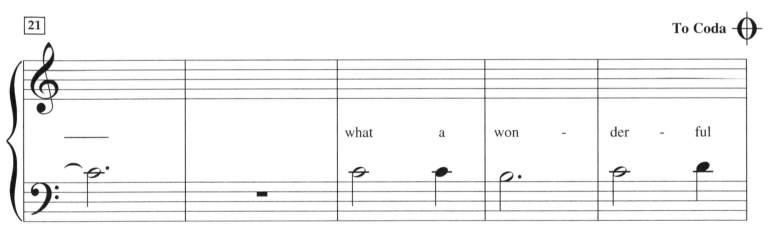

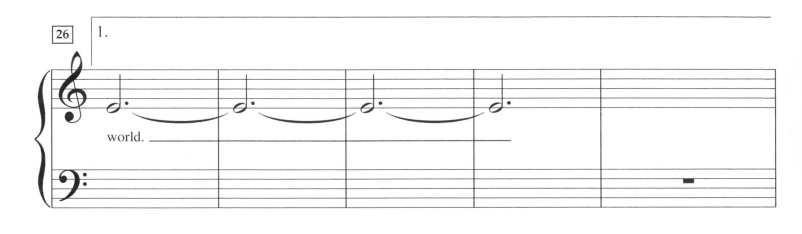

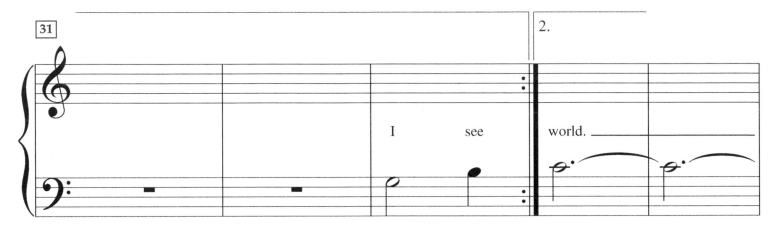

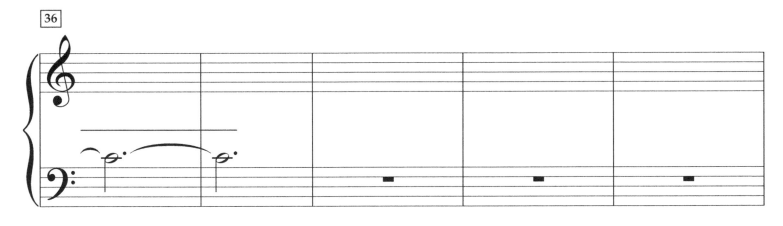

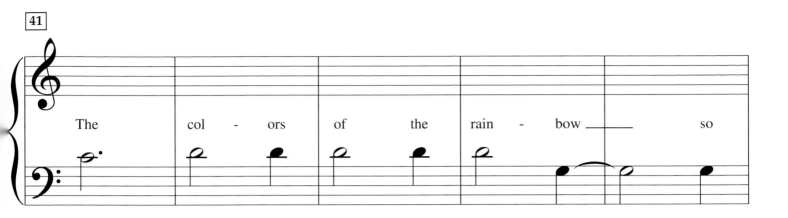

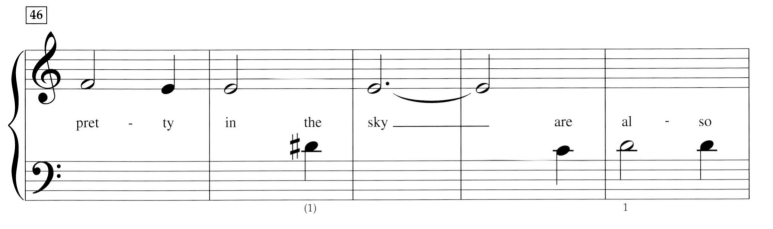

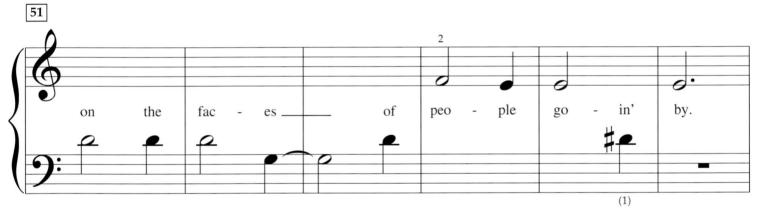

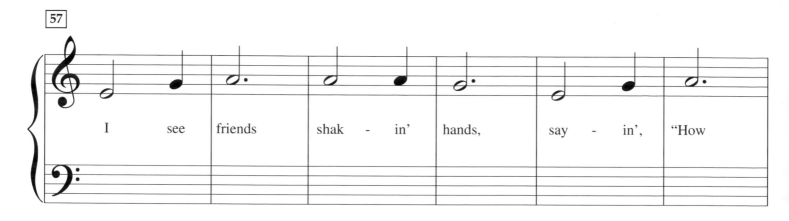

I see friends shak - in' hands, say - in', "How

do you do?" _____ They're real - ly say - in', ___

D.S. al Coda

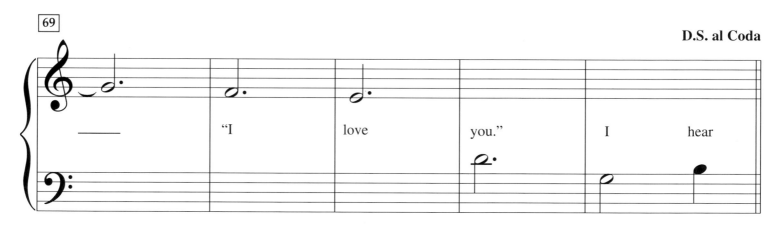

___ "I love you." I hear

D.S. al Coda

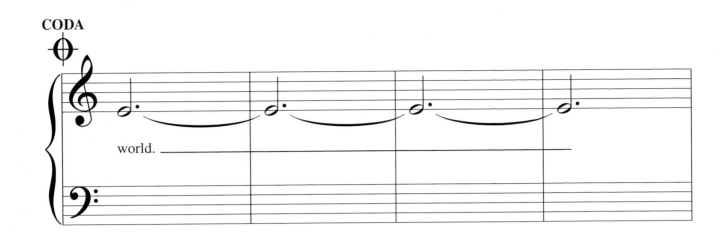

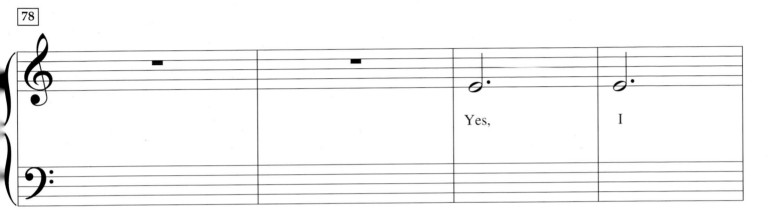

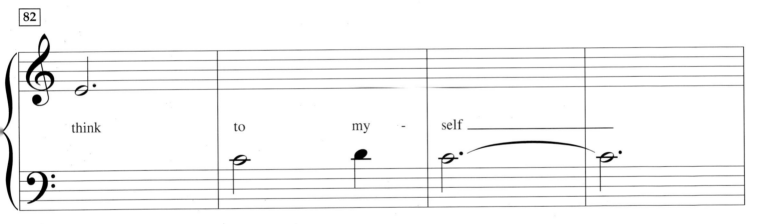

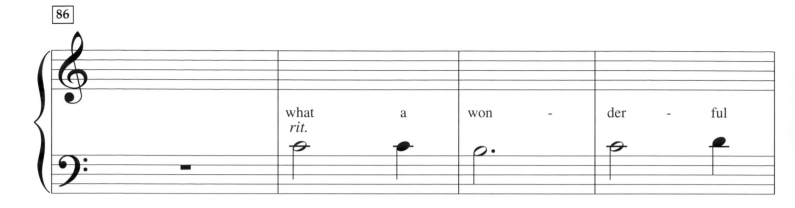

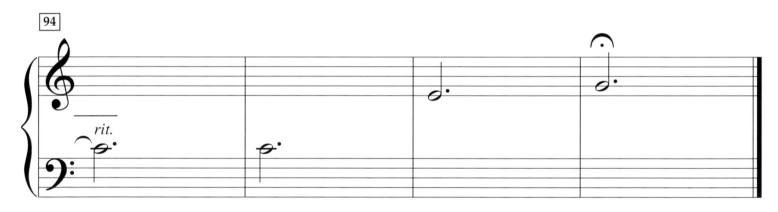

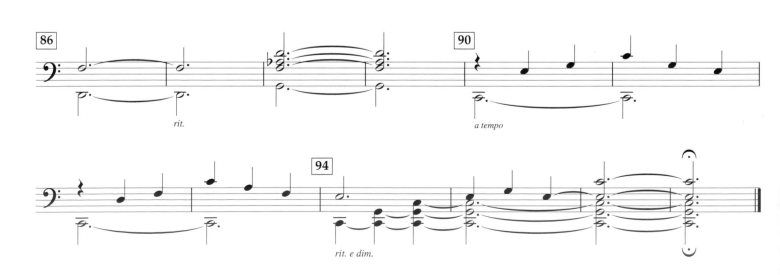